The
Micmac

**How Their Ancestors Lived
Five Hundred Years Ago**

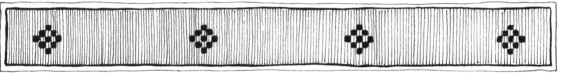

by Ruth Holmes Whitehead
and Harold McGee

illustrations by
Kathy Kaulbach

NIMBUS
PUBLISHING
LIMITED

For Rhonda Simon
and Michael Christmas

The children of *Mi'kmaq*

The Micmac
How Their Ancestors Lived
Five Hundred Years Ago
Copyright 1983
Text Ruth Holmes Whitehead
and Harold McGee
Illustrations Kathy R. Kaulbach

ISBN 0-920852-21-1 (paperback)
ISBN 0-920852-23-8 (hardcover)
Printed and bound in Canada
Published by:
Nimbus Publishing Limited
P.O. Box 9301, Station A
Halifax, N.S.   B3K 5N5

Canadian Cataloguing in Publication Data
Whitehead, Ruth Holmes
The Micmac:
How their ancestors lived five hundred years ago

For use in schools.
ISBN 0-920852-21-1

1. Micmac Indians. 2. Indians of North
America – Atlantic Provinces. * I. McGee,
Harold Franklin, 1945 – II. Title.

E99.M6W54   971.5'00497   C83-098384-8

Contents

Introduction

Five hundred years ago, the first European explorers sailed across the Atlantic Ocean to the shores of an unknown continent. In the north, between the mouth of the St. Lawrence River and the southern end of the Bay of Fundy (see map page 2), they found the land already occupied by a people now called the Micmac. The name Micmac comes from their word *nikmaq*, which means 'my kin-friends'. The Micmac used this word as a greeting, when speaking to the newcomers from Europe. Later the French adopted the term, and began addressing these Indian friends and allies as *nikmaqs*. Over the years, the word came to be written as 'Micmac'.

The Micmac, who referred to themselves as 'The People', lived along the seacoasts and rivers of what we now call the Maritime provinces. In their big canoes they traded and raided down the New England coast, up the St. Lawrence River, and north into Labrador and probably into Newfoundland.

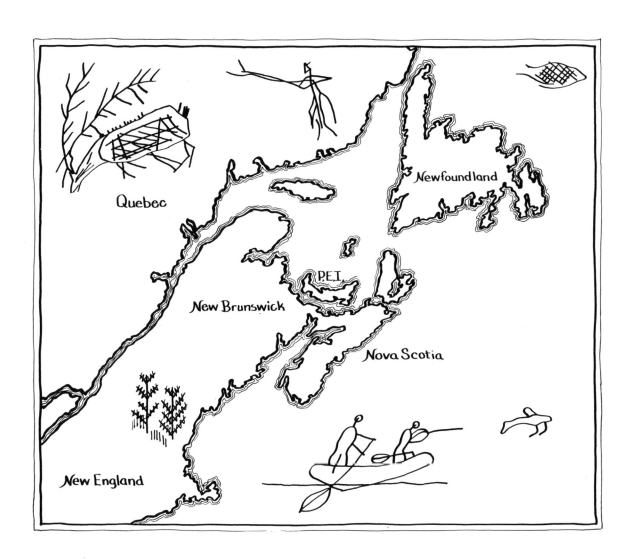

No one knows when the Micmac began moving into the Maritimes. Archaeologists who study the prehistory of this area are still trying to solve that mystery. We do know that there were people living here about 10,500 years ago. They could not have been here much earlier than 12,000 years ago because this part of Canada was still covered by glacial ice. Only after the glaciers had retreated enough for plants and animals to return, did the people come, following the herds of game.

Since that time many changes have occurred. The actual shape of the land is different, and many of its old coastlines are now underwater. There are also differences in the kinds of plants and animals in the region. The way of life of its human inhabitants has altered a number of times throughout this 10,500 year period, as new people have moved into the Maritimes.

While we do not know everything about the people who were here during that period, we do know that the Micmac had occupied the land before the first visitors from Europe arrived. There are still Micmac people living here today. This book tells the story of how the ancestors of the modern Micmac lived, five hundred years ago.

Map: The known world of the Micmac. They lived along the coasts of the Maritime provinces and travelled throughout this region.

Abundant Forest, Rivers of Fish

Five hundred years ago, the climate was much like it is today: cool damp summers, months of sun and fog, and winters which varied from cold and snowy to those where the ground was bare and temperatures often above freezing.

The environment in which the Micmac lived, however, was really very different from today's. Now there are large areas cleared of trees for pastures and fields and for towns and cities. Five hundred years ago the land was a forest filled with birch, maple, beech, oak, pine, spruce and fir trees. These provided bark for houses, canoes and containers, roots for binding, and wood for fuel as well as for many of the tools used by the Micmac. The forest was also home to many animals. Here were found bear, moose, porcupine, hare, grouse, and passenger pigeon. Along the lakes and streams of the interior there lived beaver, muskrat, raccoon and otter. The only clearings were natural meadows, marshes and bogs, or sections burnt over by forest fires. These open areas were important to the Micmac because here they found useful plants. Food plants like the groundnut, cranberry, blueberry, raspberry and strawberry grew in these sunny unforested places. Plants used in medicines or for making baskets and mats also came from these places. Some birds nested in these open areas and often moose or caribou fed there.

Plants, birds, fish and other animals provided for the needs of the Micmac.

Moose, caribou, beaver and other animals were much more common then. The rivers were so filled with fish in the spring and fall that they looked more like rivers of fish than of water. The fish were larger, too. Sturgeon often weighed 400 kg or more, while today a large one is about 100 kg. There were so many pigeons in the sky that they sometimes blocked the sun, like a large cloud. The passenger pigeon is now extinct, but there were once millions of them in the land of the Micmac. Huge herds of seal and walrus used to sun themselves and give birth to their young along the shores of the Maritime provinces; now the walrus are gone and seals are present only in small numbers.

It was along the shores of the bays, coves and rivers that the Micmac found the greatest amount of food and other materials for their needs. Here the people spent the largest part of the year. From the shallow waters they took shellfish: clams, mussels, whelks, periwinkles, squid, crabs and lobsters; and fish: flounder, smelt, shad, skate, salmon and eels. Geese, ducks and other waterbirds fed and nested close by. In deeper water the Micmac fished for porpoise, sturgeon, swordfish and the smaller whales. They hunted seals and collected birds' eggs on nearby islands.

On land, they could find most of the plants and animals they needed without having to go very far from the sea. In the late spring and fall, however, they left their coastal homes to go upstream to narrow places on the rivers where the community gathered to trap salmon and eels. They also moved into the interior for a brief period during the winter when fresh food was scarce on the coast.

Animal persons, plant persons

Because the environment was a rich one, most of what the Micmac required for daily living could be obtained from the local area. They learned the habits of the animals and the relationship between plants and animals. Since most of the things they made and all the food they ate came from these living beings whom they knew so well, the Micmac developed a respect for life. They thought of these plants and animals – and even some minerals – as persons with whom they could communicate.

A young girl is dreaming about plant persons. The groundnut on her left provided food from its pods, leaves and the tubers on its roots. Next to it is sweet-flag, with the long straight leaves. Its root was made into medicine. On the far right are cattails. Their leaves were woven, and the roots and pollen eaten. The girl's fingers reach out to pick the leaves of native tobacco, to be dried and smoked. Below that is the big-leaved bloodroot plant; its root was used as a dye. Underneath it are the tiny leaves and flowers of Labrador tea, a good drink. The last plant, close to her right side, is Indian hemp. Its stalk was crushed and the fibres made into twine and rope.

This belief affected the manner in which they hunted and used animals and plants. For instance, when they gathered a medicinal plant, they might speak to it and thank it for having shown them the season to collect it and how to use it as medicine.

Animals which were killed for food and for skins were believed to be giving up their lives so that the people could live. The Micmac developed rituals and an etiquette to show their respect for this exchange of lives. One such ritual was to hang the bones of slain animals in trees or place them in rivers and thus prevent dogs from gnawing on them. The Micmac believed that the souls of animals honoured in this way would choose to be reborn near their bones. If the bones were shown any disrespect, the souls would leave the region and the people would go hungry.

This belief about plant and animal persons prevented the Micmac from wasting the natural resources. They did not gather or hunt more than they needed to survive comfortably. They saw themselves as one of many different kinds of persons all of whom had to live in the same environment in harmony. They were a part of the complex ecological fabric, but they were not its tailors.

In the Micmac view of the world these plant and animal persons were very good to them. The Micmac made their rope from roots and bark, their bedding from fir boughs, their containers of wood or bark, and their canoes out of bark, wood, sap and roots. Plant persons also provided food for the people. These included the leaves, seeds and tubers of the groundnut, the roots of the cattail, the berries of numerous plants. Most of the food the people ate, however, was obtained from animal persons. In addition, they made use of hides and skins for clothing and containers; the bones were used to make needles, awls and spear points; the sinews became sewing thread; oils were for flavouring food, and the feathers, shells and quills for decoration.

Herds of sea mammals

The Micmac hunted a number of sea mammals, including walrus, porpoise, small whales and grey seals. The most important was the harbour seal. Its meat was good to eat and the skin was made into moccasins and other clothing. The most important product, though, was the oily fat. Harbour-seal oil was particularly good for flavouring foods, and as a hair and body oil. The fat was boiled in water, and as the oil floated to the surface, it was ladled into moose bladders for storage. Harbour seals could be hunted most of the year. Large herds of several hundred animals would sun themselves on sandy beaches in narrow coves. The Micmac approached them quietly by canoe and speared the seals in the shallow water as they attempted to get out to sea.

Men stand in an icy stream, waiting to spear salmon as they pass.

about the canoe. The harpooner would not strike until the sturgeon swam in such a way as to show the small soft scales on its stomach, for the back of the sturgeon is covered with bony plates that a Micmac harpoon could not pierce. When the fish was speared, it took off at great speed; the paddler had to be very skillful to keep the canoe from capsizing. Imagine the wild boat ride those two would have!

The sturgeon tired quickly, however, and the hunters then hauled it alongside their canoe. Since the fish could be as long as the canoe, they towed the fish to shore rather than pulling it into the boat. The sturgeon not only provided food and adventure but hours of entertainment, as the hunters would tell and retell the story of these nighttime hunts.

In the spring, fish which normally live in the sea began to move into the rivers, swimming up rapids and over small falls to lay their eggs in fresh water. Salmon and other large fish were sometimes speared at night, by torch-light, in the pools where they rested. They also were trapped at fish weirs. Men and women worked together to block the passage of the fish by

Fish as long as a canoe

Sturgeon were usually hunted at night. Two men would fish from a canoe; one sat in the stern and paddled, the other stood in the bow with a birchbark torch and a harpoon. The fish would be attracted to the light and swim

building a dam or weir of rocks, wood and shrubs at a narrow shallow place on a river. They left one small opening through which the water poured, and the salmon would attempt to jump it. On the other side would be a large net

or loosely-woven basket into which the jumping fish would fall. Three or four times a day the net would be emptied. In the fall, when the fish were returning to the sea, this net would be placed on the opposite side of the weir.

While there would certainly be fresh salmon eaten at these times, most

---

The fish which the men have caught are split and hung on the smoking racks. The women build a smouldering fire underneath, and then cover the racks to keep the smoke in. This preserves the fish.

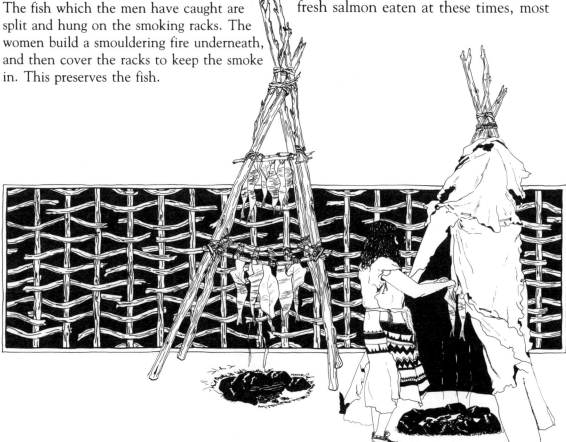

of the fish would be smoke-dried for later use. After the fish were cleaned, they were split and hung on a rack over a very smoky fire, and then these racks were covered with hides which kept in the smoke. Moose, eels, shellfish, bear, geese, and caribou were also preserved by smoking.

Calling the moose

Of the land mammals hunted by the Micmac, the moose was the biggest. In the summer, hunters would stalk moose and shoot them with arrows. Since a single arrow would not kill such a large animal, they followed it, shooting it when they could, and sometimes driving it near to their wigwam site. It might take a day or more for a large moose to die.

In the fall mating season, hunters would attempt to lure moose by using birchbark moosecalls to imitate a cow moose. A number of hunters would wait in ambush with arrows and lances; when the moose came within striking distance all the hunters would shoot their arrows and use their lances. In the winter, the hunters used dogs and wore snowshoes when stalking a moose. The best winter weather for hunting was when there was a great deal of snow. The heavy moose would sink in the snow and become tired very quickly because it could not run easily. The dogs used by the Micmacs were fairly small and lightweight and ran on top of the snow to annoy and hinder the moose. The hunters, with the aid of their snowshoes, could move fairly quickly on the snow as well. Their arrows and lances put an end to the animal.

After the kill, the women butchered the moose and hauled the cut-up carcass back to the wigwam. If the moose was killed some distance from home they might set up a temporary shelter and then camp at the kill-site for a few days. Women cut the meat into long strips for smoking. Fat, meat and berries were stuffed into the intestines, then hung in a smoky place in the wigwam for later use. However, the most welcome part of the moose was the creamy white fat that could be taken from the bones. The women would break up the bones with stone hammers and place the crushed pieces in the large wooden kettles used for preparing their soups and stews. They would heat the bone-and-water mixture by placing red-hot rocks into the kettle. The fat floated to the top and was then ladled into birchbark containers to cool. This fat was used to season food and, since it was a quick source of energy, it was sometimes eaten by itself. Large boxes of fat were given as gifts to show special respect or affection for someone.

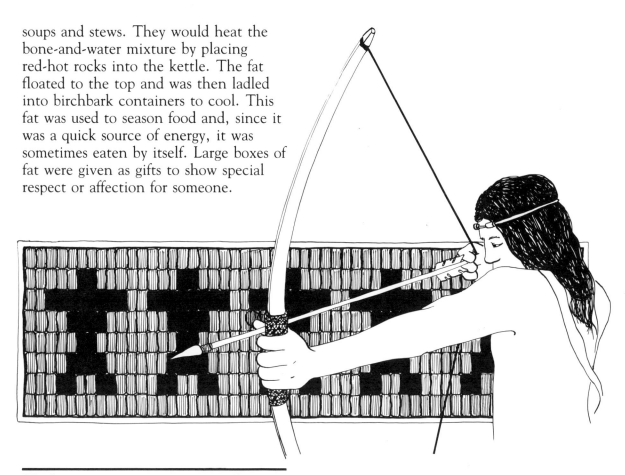

The bow was an important weapon because it allowed a hunter to bring down game from a distance.

Hot soup and roast meat

Birds were an important source of food which children could help provide. In addition to the numerous eggs that were collected, children would catch grouse with a loop-snare by sneaking up on a bird, slipping a cord loop over its head and pulling tight. Children would approach wild geese as they were feeding in a meadow and club them with sticks.

Adults usually hunted geese at night. Two or three men in a canoe would drift silently into the middle of a flock of sleeping birds; then they would light birchbark torches and make a lot of noise. The startled geese would awaken and fly into the air. In their confusion they would circle around the bright torches. The men would club the birds, then wring their necks. The Micmac could fill a large canoe in a night in this way. After having feasted on fresh roast goose, they would smoke the rest of the meat.

Smoked foods were eaten without cooking; most food was boiled, however. This was done in a kettle made from a large hardwood log. The log was hollowed out by charring the wood, then chopping out the burnt part until the hole was deep enough. These kettles were so heavy that the Micmac made one for each place where they spent a lot of time. They would have a kettle at their coastal site and at the up-river places where they trapped salmon and eels. To cook food, the kettle was filled with water and hot stones were dropped in using a pair of wooden tongs. The heat from the stones brought the water

to a boil. Then the food that was to be cooked was added. When done, the soup or stew would be served in a wooden or bark dish.

Sometimes food was roasted. Meat or fish would be stuck on a sharp stick and placed near the fire until it was done, or small pieces would be placed on a grill of green wood and put directly on the coals. Larger pieces of meat were cooked on a rotisserie. This was a device by which meat was evenly roasted without having to be closely watched. It was made by passing a cord over a bar above the fire and attaching the loose ends to a skewer stuck through the meat. The skewer was twisted – much as we wind up a child's swing – and released. The meat would rotate for a long while, first one way, then the other, until it was cooked on all sides.

Two ways of cooking: roasting meat on a rotisserie over the fire, and stewing meat in a large wooden 'kettle'. The woman is dropping in hot rocks to make the stew boil.

Family and Community

Micmac communities ranged in size from two hundred to perhaps eight hundred related people – the size of a small village today. Not all these people lived together in one place. In order to make the best use of the rich environment in which they lived, the community spaced its wigwam sites several kilometres apart along the shores of bays, coves and rivers, making sure each was near fresh drinking water and firewood. One or two families would live at each of these sites.

Although plants and animals were more plentiful in the past, these were not often all found together. For example, the Micmac could not hunt geese in the same places that they hunted seals. Therefore families traded with one another for the things they did not have. Sometimes they would give their extra food to the headman of the community, who would see to it that everyone had enough to eat. In these ways, everyone got all they needed.

There were a few jobs that required the help of a larger number of people, such as trapping the great runs of salmon or eels. At these times everyone in the community would get together for a week or two. This would be a time for festivities, visiting with friends, courting, and meeting to make important decisions.

Linked by kinship, friendship and trade

Certain people of the community were respected for their workmanship, for their knowledge or for their ability to speak well. Children might be sent to stay with them to learn a special skill. At the settlements of these respected people, the community would gather for its festive occasions. Here the community decisions would be made. These decisions might include determining who would look after newly orphaned children; where along the bay a recently married couple should set up their wigwam; when some of the men would go trading with distant groups; or whether they should make peace with a community with whom they had been feuding. Men discussed the issues among themselves, and then talked about them with their families. Then the men met again and after much discussion one person, usually the respected relative at whose wigwam they were meeting, would express the decision in such a way that everyone agreed to it.

At some of these gatherings, there were visitors from neighbouring communities or from distant tribes. Micmac villages were linked to one another by kinship, friendship and trade; and to other peoples by trade and alliances. These alliances were made to establish and maintain peace. The Micmac were on friendly terms with the Montagnais on the north shore of the St. Lawrence River, and with the Malecite and Penobscot to the west in New Brunswick and Maine. With them they traded copper and a type of stone for making tools, receiving in return other types of useful stone, maize and shell beads. Although the Micmac sometimes traded with Indian groups to the south-west, they also fought with them. Other enemies were the Inuit who lived much further south then than they do now, and the Iroquoian peoples to the west. These wars and raids were often waged to avenge relatives killed in earlier wars, and were really more like feuds.

Peace in the family

It was common for a wigwam site to be occupied by two or more related families. The closest family tie was between sisters or brothers, so that two sisters and their husbands and children, or two brothers and their wives and children, might choose to live at the same place. In the case of the women, it meant that they would have helpful and pleasant company while the men were away hunting. For the men it meant that they had a work group who got along well with one another and who understood each other's habits – something that was important when hunting silently.

Some men took more than one wife. This gave them more relatives who could help them when they needed it, and it enabled them to have more children. So some wigwam sites had a large group of people living at them, especially those of the highly respected people who had other children living with them as well as their own family.

In order for all these people at a site to get along with one another, there were rules of etiquette which everyone followed. Respect was shown to people older than oneself. There were even special words for elder brother or elder sister. **Inside the wigwam, each person had their own special place.** Women and girls were on one side; men and boys were on the other. The parents were at the back of the wigwam, the youngest children were next to them, and the oldest were near the doorway. If a person wanted to be left alone he moved against the wigwam wall. The others would not bother or talk to this person until he moved more to the centre of the wigwam, near the firepit. By showing respect for elders and by honouring others' rights to privacy, the Micmac kept peace in the family.

When people visited each other, they often gathered around the wigwam fire to listen to stories.

Children growing and learning

The birth of a child was an occasion for rejoicing. The mother washed and wrapped her new baby in soft robes, which she had painted with protective magic signs. Then she laid the baby in the wooden carrier carved with beautiful and intricate designs by its father, and she laced up the carrier strings to keep the infant snug and safe inside.

Until the child could walk, it would see the world from the back of its mother or elder sisters. While the mother worked, the carrier might be hung to swing gently from the branch of a tree or a pole inside the wigwam, out of harm's way. Bigger children would play with the baby, sitting next to it to fan away the mosquitoes or tickle it with a feather, teaching it words. Thus, from birth, children were included in all aspects of family life. Their parents loved them dearly, and invited the whole community to a birth feast. They often celebrated the first step and the first tooth with another feast.

A baby on its mother's back, laced into the wooden carrier. This kept the infant safe and close to its mother while she worked.

Children learned by watching and listening and by imitation. Almost as soon as they could toddle around the camp, little boys were playing with toy spears and tiny bows, practising the arts of stalking and trapping, studying the tracks and calls of mammals and birds as they tagged after their fathers and uncles or brothers.

Children learned by watching. Here a mother teaches her daughter how to paint on birchbark, using a bone tool.

A small girl crawling into her mother's lap as she wove reeds into baskets might be given a handful of reeds of her own, and shown how to plait them. Later her mother would teach her how to gather reeds, how to dry them and where and when dye-plants might be found to colour the reeds. As a girl grew older, she learned the seasons and uses for hundreds of plants, and she might live for a time with a great-aunt who could tell her how to prepare medicines from bark, leaves, seeds and roots. Both boys and girls had to know how to make, repair, load, paddle and carry a canoe. All these things and more they learned as they helped with daily chores, or listened to elders telling stories about why the world was so.

The Micmac used myths and stories to teach children the truth about the world as they saw it: about the properties of plant and animal persons and their relationships with human beings; about the ways in which people either get along or fight with one another. Through these dramatic and humorous stories the children learned about life, and about the history, customs and manners of their people.

Preparing a marriage and a feast

Girls were considered women of marriageable age when they became physically mature. A boy became a man in the eyes of the community when he had killed his first moose; he was then allowed to marry. A young man went to the parents of the girl he liked, and asked permission to live with them for a trial period of one to three years. During that time he hunted and fished for her family, and made all the equipment that a man would need to support and care

A young women dressed for her marriage feast. Her white robe is painted with red and black designs, and has mussel shells and copper dangles sewn on the front. Her braids and face are also painted.

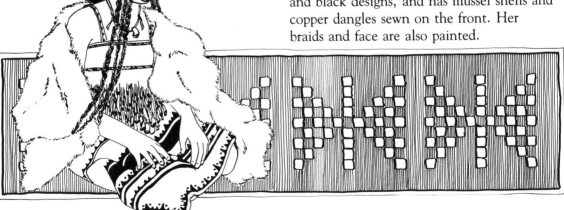

for a family of his own: tools, weapons, a sled, a canoe, snowshoe frames. His fiancée in turn demonstrated her skills: butchering his kills, cooking his food, preparing his clothes, weaving in the webbing of his snowshoes.

This trial period enabled everyone to see how they liked each other, and to judge whether the two young people were capable of performing all the tasks necessary to the survival of a household. At some point the parents met, and if the couple was willing and the families agreeable, a marriage feast was celebrated. The young man provided hundreds of kilos of food for this as a final demonstration of his worth. The eating went on for days, while stories

were told, the family histories of the couple were recited and tobacco pipes were passed around. Chanting and dancing and games added to the excitement.

After the marriage ceremony, a young couple might live alone, stay with various relatives, or go visiting for a while, as they chose. The first baby arrived, and family life began anew.

Micmac men and women cut their hair as a sign of marriage. This young man's headband is covered with bone beads, copper tubes and shells, with a blue-jay's wing on either side.

When death came, each person wished to present a brave and calm appearance as an example to others. Many people composed and sang their personal death songs celebrating events in a long and full life, of journeys by land and sea, great kills made, children borne, of special visions long remembered. They sang of enemy raids, of whales washing ashore, forest fires, the yearly breaking up of the ice, of the good taste of beaver meat and smoked eels. . . .

The funeral began with speeches and singing. If the ground were frozen when the person died, the body was preserved on a high platform out of reach of animals, until spring thaws enabled it to be buried. Each person gave presents to the dead one, supplies of fur and food and tools to keep him comfortable in the spirit world. Then the body, wrapped in robes and reed mats and cased in a shroud of birchbark, was put into the ground with its gifts.

Celebration with chanting and dancing

Both singing and dance were an important part of daily life, as well as being part of the celebration of rituals, feasts, funerals and preparations for war. Dance included mime, with the performers imitating animals so well they almost seemed to become the animal. Men dramatized their hunts or fights through dance. One of the important women's dances was about how the medicine plants came to be known. In the snake dance, a line of men and women coiled and uncoiled in the kinds of intricate circles that snakes can make.

There were only a few musical instruments, used in dance and rituals: the rattles made of fish-skin pulled over a wooden frame and filled with tiny pebbles, the bone whistles and the birchbark slabs beaten with sticks like a drum. Dancers often wore dangles of bone or moose dewclaws which clashed and clicked as they moved.

Traditional Micmac Skills

After a hunter had killed an animal, the women carefully removed its skin before butchering it. From the hides and furs of moose, caribou, beaver, bear and seal they made most of the family clothes. A skin was tied to a wooden stretching frame, and the women scraped the inside clean. If the fur was not wanted, they removed all the hair and scraped the outside. Next the skin was rubbed all over with oil or grease and a tanning substance such as animal brains, which softened and preserved the leather. The skin was worked and stretched to make it supple. Finally the whole hide was suspended over a smouldering fire and smoked to ensure that the leather stayed supple, even if it got wet later. Smoking also coloured animal hides, which are naturally creamy white; Micmac women could stain them different shades of tan, brown and black, depending on the length of time they were kept in the smoke.

Clothing

Men and women wore loincloths of soft skin, with the ends fastened to a belt at the waist. Each had a pair of leggings of thicker moosehide or sealskin for warmth, and to protect the legs from scratchy underbrush. Their moccasins were also of moose or seal leather, sewn with very fine close stitches to help keep water out. In winter, moccasins might be lined with fur and have high tops. Some were simply a long tube of skin from a moose leg, pulled off whole, then sewn up across the toe. Both men and women wore a pair of sleeves – one sleeve to cover each arm and shoulder. These were tied together at the back and front.

Each person had a blanket-sized robe of suede-like leather or rich warm beaver fur which was worn over the shoulders in winter. Women had a second robe which acted as a dress. There were two kinds of women's robes, both of which had belts at the waist and fell to below the knees. Children had similar clothing and little babies were wrapped up in the softest fox fur or in the feathered skins of swans.

For sewing, a bone awl was used to pierce the leather, but there were also needles of bone or copper. For thread, women had strands of dried animal sinew. The robes for men and women were tied rather than sewn, because they were taken off at night and used for bedcovers.

A man's ceremonial robe of white moosehide, elaborately ornamented and fringed, with a decoration of dried gull's feet. The painted animals might represent special hunts, a dream, or the man's spirit-helpers.

Decoration

A bow-loom for weaving porcupine quills, shown with a close-up of the finished weave. Woven quillwork looks a lot like woven beadwork.

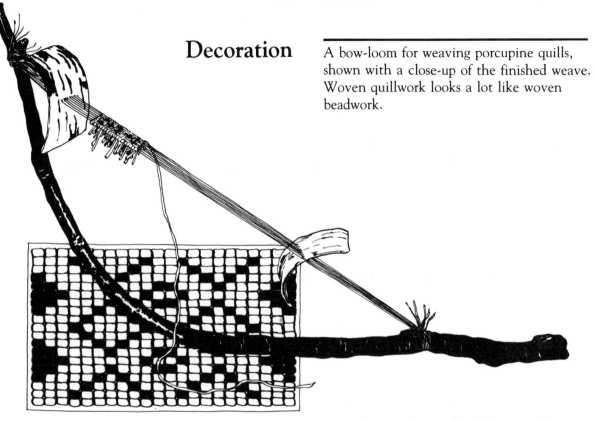

Clothing and accessories were beautifully made and decorated. Ornaments and decoration were thought to give magic protection to the wearer and to add to one's status and power. Leather was often painted; the borders of robes, the cuffs and toes of moccasins, the bottoms and sides of leggings might show bands of parallel painted lines, geometric designs like triangles, circles and scallops, or the intricate 'double-curve' motif. Robes, pouches and leggings were usually covered with wonderfully realistic pictures of animals, birds, people and monsters. To do this kind of work, women ground up mineral pigments like red or yellow ochre, chalky white shells, or charcoal. They mixed each pigment with fish roe or egg yolks to make their four traditional colours of paint: red, white, black and yellow. Sometimes a touch of blue or violet was added, perhaps obtained from blueberries. The painting tools for applying the colours were made from bone.

With plant dyes, porcupine quills were dyed red, blue, black, brown, green or gold. Together with the glistening white undyed quills, they were worked into a variety of ornamentation. Quills could be woven into long strips, like woven beadwork, then backed with leather and used as belts or cuffs or fancy panels on robes and pouches. Quill embroidery was done by folding wet quills over and under lines of stitching on the outside of the garment. Fringes were wrapped with colourful quills, and braided quill strings used as headbands.

Women also embroidered on leather with moose hair in a method called couching, in which lengths of hair were laid on the skin and then sewed down. Strips of painted hide or fur were stitched onto the clothing to make raised lines in contrasting colours. A costume might have dangles of shell, bone, stone, feathers, teeth, claws, antlers, or tiny copper cones and cylinders. This copper, called 'native copper', seems to have come from the Cape D'Or region of Nova Scotia, where it can be found in thin sheets that can be cut and hammered into shape very easily.

Both the face and hair were painted for important occasions, and often the legs, arms and chest as well. Black was for funerals and mourning, while men painted themselves red for war. For a feast, a woman might make a series of braids in her hair, colour some of them red with ochre powder, tie copper cones, shells and feathers along them, and then colour the rest of her hair or her hair-parting another shade. Dots, stripes and patches of colour decorated the face. Usually each person created his or her own design. A man might wear a headdress of bird wings or a roach of stiff moose hair dyed red. A knife in an elaborate sheath around the neck, with several pouches and a tobacco pipe hanging from the belt, completed the costume for men and women.

Micmac women painted intricate designs on their family's leggings, moccasins, sleeves and robes. Some of these designs were realistic, some were simply decorative, and others were symbolic. Their meanings are now lost. Note that the woman carries her

knife in a sheath about her neck, and the
man wears a mink-skin tobacco pouch.
Children dressed like their parents.

Wigwam means shelter

The Micmac people lived in wigwams. Wigwam is a Micmac word which means a dwelling, or shelter. The people knew how to make a number of different shapes and sizes of wigwams. The conical type, with one door and a fireplace in the centre, was the most common, but there was also a longer A-frame shape with a door and a fire at each end. The V-type wigwam had a triangular floor-plan. It looked like a V from above, with a door at the wide end. There was also a rounded hut, which resembled a bowl turned upside down. All of these dwellings were built by putting up a structure of poles, then covering these with bark or hide or reed mats, or a combination of these. A birchbark covering was best, because it was waterproof and insects did not eat it.

The V-type wigwam could hold more people. It had a bark cover with two ridgepoles. The firepit was near the door.

To put up a conical wigwam with a birchbark cover, the women first made its frame. They cut five to ten long spruce poles and tied them together at their tops with lengths of tough spruce root. Standing the poles up, they then spread them apart at the bottom until the logs formed a cone shape the size of the wigwam they wanted. Next a thick sapling was bent into a hoop and lashed to the inside of this frame, at about the height of a man's head. The hoop kept the poles from slipping inward or outward.

A cone-shaped wigwam was the easiest kind to erect. It had a birchbark cover over a wooden frame, a heavy leather hide for a door, and a firepit in the center.

The women building the wigwam filled in the spaces between their first frame with smaller poles, which were tied at intervals to the hoop. These poles were not as long as the main spruce logs, and did not touch them at any point. They rested only on the hoop. After this task was done, the dwelling was ready to be covered. Long sheets of birchbark, which were kept warm and wet so they would not tear, were sewed onto the frame like big shingles, starting at the bottom. Each bark piece overlapped the one below it, so that water could not get in. To sew the bark together, and to tie it to the frame, women used more spruce root. This time it was split into smaller widths, and the bark removed. Using a bone awl, they punched tiny holes in the birchbark, and threaded the root through.

The birchbark covered a conical structure only up to the tops of the second set of poles. A wigwam of this sort was left open at the peak for smoke to escape. In bad weather someone climbed up a log ladder and put a collar of bark over the smoke-hole. Inside, the people were warm and dry. A rock fireplace in the centre provided heat, light and a place for cooking. This firepit had an edging of sand around it, for safety. The rest of the wigwam had a floor-covering of fragrant fir twigs, over which the women laid mats of woven reeds and fur robes. In winter more reed mats lined the wigwam walls, providing insulation. Firewood and water were stored near the door. Other family possessions might be hung or stored on the floor along the walls.

There were conical wigwams which held up to thirty people. Usually, however, an A-frame or V-type would be erected to house a large group. An A-frame had two long poles at either end which were tied together at their tops and which supported the ridgepole. Other poles were laid with their tops lashed to the ridgepole, and then a bark cover was put on. Holes were left at the top on each end directly above the fireplace, to let the smoke escape. The V-type was similar, but had two ridgepoles, joined by a cross-braced bar at the open end of the V. The rounded huts were usually long saplings bent over at the tops, tied down and covered. The Micmac frequently made

this shape when they wanted a small sweat-lodge – the little huts they used for taking steam baths.

A wigwam's bark cover was light in weight and could be removed, rolled up (after being warmed and wetted again), then carried along with the people as they travelled. Women decorated these covers on the outside with painted pictures of animals, birds and fish, so that in addition to being easily built, portable, warm and dry, the birchbark wigwam was an attractive sight.

Remember that 'wigwam', or *wikuom* as the Micmac now spell it, is the correct term. The word 'tipi' or 'teepee' comes from a different Indian language, so it is not really accurate to call a Micmac dwelling a tipi.

Women warmed the birchbark for their wigwam covers before sewing and attaching each sheet to the frame. This helped keep the bark from splitting.

A Micmac family could travel the deep seas and shallow streams in their birchbark canoe. Notice how the canoe sides curve up in the centre to keep out waves.

Canoe

The canoe and snowshoe were both North American Indian inventions. These two items, together with the toboggan and sled, allowed the Micmac people to travel in winter and summer. Both canoe and snowshoe are so perfectly adapted to the land and climate that they were immediately adopted by the European explorers and settlers who later came to this continent. Their basic forms remain unchanged and in use today.

The birchbark canoe was probably the most impressive Micmac construction. It could be taken far out to sea or up shallow streams and down whitewater rapids. In a country of hills and forests where water is the only road, the canoe was the best way to travel. It could carry great loads, but was light enough for one or two people to portage from waterway to waterway, to take around dangerous waterfalls, or to pole upstream. Thus a family in a canoe could travel far through the interior, using connected rivers, lakes and streams as their highway.

The Micmac canoe ranged in length from three to eight metres. Its high ends and the sides which curved upwards towards the centre kept it from taking on lots of water in rough seas. This shape was distinctive; it marked the canoe as having been made by a Micmac and nobody else.

To build a canoe, men looked for big White Birch trees and cut the heavy bark from them as single sheets, as high up as possible before the branches began. These sheets of bark were placed on the ground and then folded up over the wooden frame of the craft. Split spruce root was used to sew the bark together and to bind it to the frame. Sometimes the root was dyed different colours. Where the bark had been joined, the seams were caulked with spruce gum to make the boat waterproof.

Paddles were made of beech, maple or ash. They had blades as long as a man's arm, and were often decorated with carved designs.

The Micmac people also made hide-covered boats, using the skins of moose or caribou in place of bark. These were used as temporary craft when a canoe was not available, because the untanned skin cover rotted after a short while in the water.

Tumpline and toboggan

The people travelled on foot, or by canoe as long as the waterways were free of ice. When they had to move heavy loads on land they made use of the tumpline. This was a carrying strap; its wide centre section was worn across the forehead or chest in front, and the narrower lengths on either side were used to strap the burden onto the person's back. With a tumpline a man or woman could carry 50 to 90 kilograms.

Wooden sleds carried the family possessions or the hunter's kill smoothly over the ice. A man could make a sled in less than a day.

When winter came the people travelled on the frozen rivers and lakes, and they transported their possessions by toboggan and sled. A toboggan was made of wide flat planks split from a large Rock Maple tree trunk. It curved upward at one end, making use of the portion where a branch began to curve out from the tree. Toboggans slid easily across the ice. Sleds had runners, and were made from Rock Maple or Yellow Birch. A person could pull about 200 kilograms, or half a moose, on a sled like this.

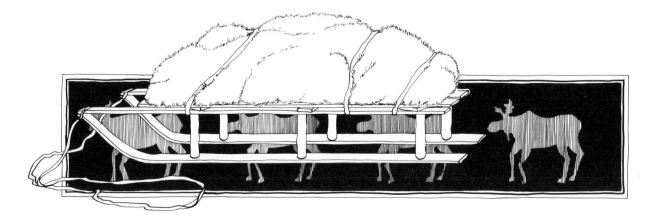

Snowshoes

In order to travel and to hunt after snowfall, snowshoes were a necessity. They spread the body's weight over a wider surface, so the wearer did not sink deeply into the snow. In some ways they resembled a tennis racquet, having a wooden frame and an inside strung with rawhide. Rawhide is the uncured skin of an animal. The Micmac took a moose or caribou hide and cut it into one long continuous narrow strip. After bending the frame of ash wood into an oval shape, the maker bound the tail ends of the frame together. Then the rawhide thong was woven with a wooden needle in-and-out through holes in the frame until the inside was filled with a rawhide mesh.

Sometimes the mesh was very closely woven; this gave more support, and was the type needed when carrying heavy loads. Sometimes the mesh was more open; this let snow fall through the webbing, and it was the type used for hunting. That way, a man chasing a moose was not slowed down by snow building up on top of his snowshoes.

In an unexpected snowstorm, the people might tie spruce branches to their feet to help them walk over the snow, or make temporary snowshoes by bending a sapling into a frame, then filling it with strips of birchwood fibre. These did not last very long. The regular snowshoe, however, was so well-designed and worked so beautifully that it is still made today, relatively unchanged.

This Micmac snowshoe has an ashwood frame and a webbing of caribou rawhide. A cord through the two centre holes was tied over the foot near the toes when in use. The background design is a closeup of the snowshoe webbing.

Tools

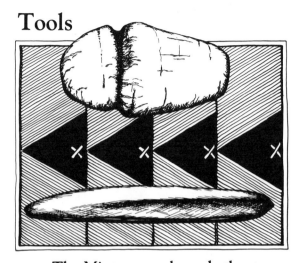

The Micmac people made the things they needed from the raw materials around them. Over the centuries their ancestors had discovered how to use animal bone, ivory, teeth, claws, sinew, hide, fur, feathers, quills, hooves and shells, clay, copper and stone; and wood, bark, roots and other plant parts. From these materials they created clothing, houses, transportation and all the tools, furnishings, weapons and toys which enabled them to live and to enjoy life. They managed to do all this without metals or machinery, relying only on their own skills and knowledge.

Traditionally, there were certain crafts and chores that were done by men and some which were women's responsibilities. Both contributed their special skills, although each probably knew enough about the other's work to cope in emergencies. Women usually built the family wigwam, for example, but a hunter alone in the woods would set up one for himself. Women sometimes made canoes, although ordinarily this would be done by a husband, father or brother. As well, some things were made by men and women together, each working on a different stage; for example for snowshoes men made the frames and weaving needles, and women produced the rawhide and wove it in.

A stone axe-head and an adze, used for cutting and working wood. The Micmac made tools like these by pecking and grinding chunks of granite or sandstone.

Men hunted, fished and fought, and they made the tools and weapons necessary to do all those things. They worked with wood, bone, antler and stone, fashioning log kettles, baby carriers, toboggans, tobacco pipes, duck decoys and bowls and spoons. Many of the items they made were decorated with carved designs.

Axes and adzes were formed by pecking and grinding stones such as granite to a sharp edge and smooth surface. In turn, these tools were used to cut and work wood. Finer carving and gouging was done with beaver teeth – the front teeth of the beaver, which are strong enough to gnaw through trees. Sometimes the beaver tooth was sharpened to a point, to cut thin lines. The front teeth of moose and porcupine were also good woodworking tools. All three could be hafted – set in handles – to give the carver a better grip. To smooth wood and bone, the men used the sharp edges of shells, or sanded their work with grit. Holes were drilled with a bow-drill which had been filled with a stone bit.

Micmac men also made knife-blades, spear-points, arrowheads and scrapers of stone. Only certain types of rock were used, rock with a special crystalline structure, such as quartz, agate, chert and jasper. All these stones break in a very particular way when hit. A man who knew exactly where to strike the stone, and how hard to strike, would shape a rock 'core' into the form he wanted by breaking off flakes along its surface edges. This was not crudely done. It took years of careful practice to learn. The Micmac tool-kits for stone-knapping, as it is called, included hammers of various sizes made of rock or antler.

A small woodworking tool, with a sharpened beaver tooth fitted on at each end of the wooden haft.

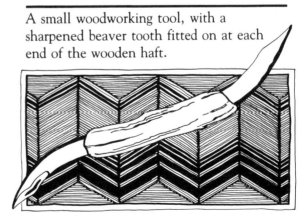

The finished knife or spear was razor-sharp and it cut like steel or broken glass. The beautiful rock from which these pieces came made them very colourful: milk-white, salmon-pink with stripes, or purple and grey.

With tools like these, men made their wooden lances with the sharp bone points for killing moose and caribou. To take sturgeon, swordfish and seals, they developed harpoons with barbed bone heads. There were fish and eel spears, called 'leisters', with a bone point in the centre and two wooden prongs on either side. The prongs spread open as the bone point passed through the body of the fish, then closed around the fish to hold it fast. Leisters came in different sizes and shapes, according to the type of fish a man was after. Men also made fishhooks of bone, wood and copper. Fish nets were probably made by both men and women.

From a rock core like the one on the left, a man could produce a number of tools, such as this knife blade and arrowhead, and these scrapers.

Men shaped and sanded their own wooden bows, then strung them with hair or sinew. Arrows with stone or bone heads, or the blunt wooden tip used to stun birds, all had a 'fletching' of eagle feathers at the end, attached with fine sinew or hemp thread, and perhaps a resin glue. The fletching helped the arrow fly straight.

For wars and raiding parties, a man armed himself with a bow, a quiver of arrows, a stone axe and a wooden club. Some of these clubs had heads of the spikey taproots of spruce trees, with part of the tree's trunk left on for a handle. Others had round heads. Wooden shields were long rectangles with a rounded top; they protected warriors from the arrows of the enemy.

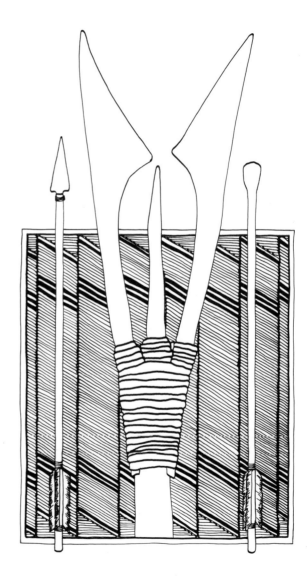

The bone-pointed arrow to the left is for killing game; the arrow on the right has a blunted wooden tip for killing birds. The fish spear has a bone point in the centre, with two wooden prongs.

Pipes and *waltes* games

Since men, women and children all smoked, pipes were very important. There was a wide assortment: pipes with stone bowls and stems, stone bowls with wooden stems, wooden bowls with wooden stems. There were pipes of lobster claws, or antler, of copper, even pipes of birchbark with maple-wood mouthpieces. For pipe-tobacco they used leaves from a native tobacco plant, and the leaves, bark and stems of bearberry, lobelia, red cornel and squawbush.

Two men playing the dice game, *waltes*. By slamming the wooden bowl down, the dice are tossed up. A third man holds the wooden counting sticks. Counting sticks and two dice can be seen in the close-up at the bottom of the picture.

A favourite dice game, called *waltes*, was played by tossing six bone or ivory dice with a wooden bowl. The game was scored by the number of decorated sides of the dice which turned up. Men made these circular dice from moose shin-bones. The decorated side was flat, the blank side was convex. *Waltes* bowls were carved from wooden burls. The score was kept with wooden counting sticks; some of these, with a greater value, had carved designs at the top. *Waltes* has been played in the Maritimes for hundreds of years, and the game is still made and played today.

Reeds, roots and porcupine quills

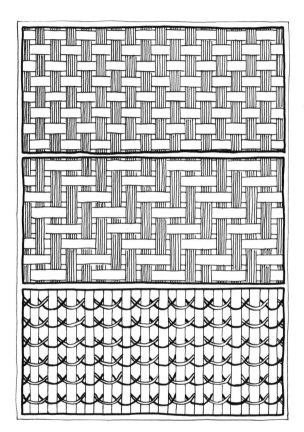

Micmac women butchered, cooked, built the wigwam, and prepared clothing and its ornamentation. They made cordage – the ropes, netting, twine, string and lashing that their families needed – and most of the containers: bowls, dishes, pots, baskets and bags.

Women were also skilled weavers. Their materials included cedar bark, basswood bark, reeds, rushes, cattails, nettles, Indian hemp, sweetgrass, spruce roots, beach grass, rawhide, tendon thread, feathers, moose hair, porcupine quills, and the skins of everything from caribou to rabbits to eels. Think about this for a minute: they had to know where and when and how to gather all these things, and how to prepare them for use. They had to learn six basic techniques of weaving with many variations for each of the different materials. Some materials could be woven three or four different ways. This is an impressive technology.

The chequer weave, the twill weave and the twine weave, all used by Micmac women.

Women gathered long green reeds in late summer or early fall. When dried and dyed, they were used to weave baskets and mats. The background design shows a twill weave in a mat of flattened reeds.

Baskets, boxes, bags and bowls

Women made all sorts of containers, too. Containers were very important to a people who had no closets, no kitchen shelves or bureaus. A people who moved regularly on foot or by canoe had to have lightweight but sturdy baskets, boxes, bags and bowls in which to store and to carry all the family possessions and food supplies. Women solved the problem by using a variety of strong but light materials.

There were bags of tanned leather or containers for which animal skin was allowed to dry into stiff rawhide. Tobacco pouches, knife sheaths, carrying sacks and quivers were a few of the items made from skin. Sometimes an animal's furred skin was taken off whole and used as a bag.

Bags were also made by weaving together flat strips of the soft inner bark of cedar or basswood trees. These containers were like stiff felt to the touch. Basswood bark strips could also be rolled into cordage and then woven. Baskets as well as bags were made of long reeds. Sometimes women flattened the reeds before weaving, or wove them together with bark twine. Sometimes twine made from Indian hemp was turned into bags by itself or used with bark or reeds. There were baskets of wood and roots, baskets of rushes, and baskets made from tough grasses.

Baskets, boxes, dishes, bowls, ladles and canoe bailers were frequently made from birchbark. Women cut the bark into a particular pattern, folded it into the shape they wanted, then sewed it together with split spruce root. A birchbark container could be stitched so tightly that it held water. It was even possible to boil water in a birchbark pot. Food was usually served in birchbark bowls and dishes, and maple sugar and syrup was stored in covered bark containers. Women decorated their barkwork by painting it, by threading porcupine quills through the root stitches, or by scraping off portions of the dark layer on one side of the bark to show a lighter layer beneath.

At one time, Micmac women made pottery from clay mixed with sand or crushed shell. However, the manufacture and use of pottery died out just before the arrival of Europeans. Both pottery and bark pots held water, but there were other containers for liquid as well. The bladders of large animals, for instance, were cleaned and used to store liquids such as seal oil – a favourite food.

The long intestines of moose or caribou became sausage casings for meat mixed with dried berries and fat. An intestine or a cougar's tail-skin with the fur left on may have been turned into a case for the hunter's bow or bowstring, which had to be kept dry in order to work.

These are only some of the clever and practical ways in which Micmac men and women used the materials around them, to make all the things they needed: food, clothing, warmth, shelter, transportation, tools and furnishings.

Women made birchbark bowls and containers, sewn with spruce root and reinforced by a wooden rim. Men made conical birchbark moosecalls and carved the wooden spoons. In the background is a detail of the designs scratched on the small container.

Fire was a necessity of life – for warmth, cooking, and the preservation of food and skins by smoking. The Micmac struck sparks by hitting chert (a stone related to flint) with iron pyrites. The sparks caught fire in dry rotted wood called punk, which the people used as tinder. This was similar to the flint-and-steel method used at one time in Europe to start fires.

The heat created by friction was high enough to cause tinder to burst into flame. A bow-drill or other device for making friction was set up and packed around with tinder, to light fires. These methods took time, however, so when a Micmac family moved camp or went on a journey, they might carry hot coals from their last fire in a clamshell lined with clay and tied shut. Punk stuffed around the coals kept the embers fed until the new fire was laid and ready to be lit.

Medicine and Magic

There was little sickness among the Micmac before the introduction of European diseases in the 1500s. When people did feel ill, they were treated with herbal medicines. More serious were injuries caused by accidents. These could take weeks to heal. Sometimes a person might feel that recurring illness or injury was the result of someone bewitching them.

From childhood, men and women heard the stories of how the various plant medicines came to be known. Often the stories would tell of a stranger who came to visit a particular settlement where there was sickness. As the stranger was shown hospitality and goodwill, he would reveal that he was really a plant person disguised as a human. He would then change form and show the people how the plant looked at each season. He told when the plant should be gathered and how to prepare it for use as medicine. Most of these medicines were brewed as teas.

Although everyone had some medicinal knowledge, there were people who were especially respected for their skills as curers. Some of the plants they used were sweetflag, strawberry, teaberry, pine, and yellow birch.

Injury as the result of accident was more common than sickness. The Micmac were very skillful in setting bones and in treating wounds. Sprains would be relieved by binding the injured joint with fresh eelskin. As the eelskins dried, they tightened like an elastic bandage. A broken bone would be set and the arm or leg covered with soft moss soaked in the sap of the fir tree. Then birchbark was wrapped around the limb and wooden splints tied on. After several weeks rest, the broken bone would have healed. Fir balsam was used to cover a wound to stop the bleeding and seal the cut. Everything the Micmac needed to treat an injury was generally close at hand. Because treatment had to be immediate in the case of injury, this was knowledge that everyone shared.

As in our time, there were things which caused emotional stress. If these feelings lasted very long, a person might become very depressed and not talk to others. In mild cases, the unhappy person's relatives and friends tried to cheer him up by having a party where people sang, ate good food and told funny stories.

In severe cases of stress, whether caused by recurring illness, injury, misfortune or depression, a person might feel he was being bewitched. Some enemy was trying to do him harm. At this point, a *puoin* was asked to help the victim. This was a person who had the spiritual power and knowledge necessary to cure those who had been bewitched. The *puoin* spent a lot of time with the sick person, asking him questions about his dreams and recent activities. He chanted special songs and danced; sometimes he massaged or blew upon the patient. As the chanting and dance reached its peak, the *puoin* struggled to pull an object which contained the evil sent by the witch out of the patient, or from the ground nearby. He then destroyed this. The sick person, seeing the cause of his illness made into something real which could be removed from him and smashed, felt his fear and anxiety leave him, and began to recover. The *puoin* might then talk to him about how to avoid such attacks in the future. A *puoin* had to have special insight into behaviour and the personal power needed to perform these healing rituals. This was a gift only a few people had, so the *puoin* was among the most respected members of the community.

The Micmac believed that all living things, and some non-living things, had souls. Although each soul had its own body in which it normally lived, especially powerful souls could cause their normal bodies to change shape. Anything that had a soul could communicate with others. Just as someone has special human friends, some Micmac had special non-human friends. These were called 'spirit-helpers' because, just like human friends, when someone needed help these non-human friends provided it. This belief also meant that most Micmac behaviour involved what we think of as religious or spiritual attitudes. For important occasions they had particular rituals, but everyday activities were all forms of religious devotion and respect for life.

This man's spirit-helper is a bear. The bond between a person and his spirit-helper was very strong. It was said that powerful people could even take on the shape of a spirit-helper.

Whole communities began to die

The life of the Micmac as we have described it did not last. With the first European fishermen came drastic changes. Metals replaced stone, bone and wooden tools. Cotton and wool, which the women now decorated with glass beads and ribbon, replaced quilled and painted leather clothing. The gun replaced the arrow and the spear. **All the choices were made willingly, because the people preferred the new materials and techniques to the old.**

Some changes which the Europeans brought about were unexpected; many were harmful changes. In order to trade for all these new items, the people had to have something the Europeans wanted in return, and the Europeans usually wanted furs, the skins of small animals like sable, mink, otter, muskrat and beaver. This meant the Micmac had to change their dwelling places, since animals like these lived inland, along the smaller streams. So much time was spent there trapping that the people had little left over in which to hunt the coastal animals they needed for food. They came to depend on European food – on dried peas and dried fruit, stale flour and hard biscuit.

The most terrible change was caused by European disease. The Micmac had no natural immunity to even the mildest cold virus, let alone to typhoid fever, measles, diphtheria and smallpox. Those diseases had been unknown in the New World until the Europeans arrived. Whole communities began to die; often everyone got sick at the same time and there was no one well enough to nurse the rest, or even to bury the dead. **Within one hundred years after European contact, seventy-five percent of the Micmac population was gone.** This had a tremendous effect on the religious beliefs, the social life, and the emotional state of the survivors. Much knowledge and history was lost during this time, because there were few grandparents left alive to pass tradition on, and few children left to listen. It must have seemed like the end of the world, and in a way it was; things would never be the same again.

After 1600 the French and the English became involved in a struggle for ownership and control of Micmac territory. The Micmac thought of the land as theirs, but because they felt more threatened by the English, they accepted weapons from the French, helping them in their wars against the English. This fighting went on for a hundred and fifty years, and many people on each side were killed.

When peace was finally made about 1760, the English were in control of Micmac lands, although this area had not been bought or captured from them. As large numbers of English-speaking people began to settle in the Maritimes, the Micmac could no longer use all the places where their ancestors had camped. The English settlers valued the good coastal sites for the same reasons the Micmac did, so they took them; the Micmac were pushed back into the forest where the living was poor, or were encouraged to move to reserves set aside for them.

The government expected the Micmac to settle down there and learn to farm. Reserve lands were often unfit for farming, however, and in the early 1800s there was a series of crop diseases and droughts that ruined farmers all over the Maritimes. Many Micmac families had to leave their small farms and return to the forests to hunt for food. But the forests were shrinking, and so were the numbers of animals and fish. Many people starved, and smallpox and tuberculosis raged through their camps. The 19th century was a harsh time for most Micmac.

Struggle

Still the people struggled to survive. The men adapted their skills at woodworking to become carpenters, coopers and craftsmen. The women developed the art of making porcupine-quill mosaics on birchbark, and sold these as well as their fancy beadwork on cloth. Both men and women made splint baskets to trade for food or a little cash. With their knowledge of the woods, Micmac men were hired as guides, loggers and mail-carriers between settlements. Surviving families took in the orphans, invalids and old people. They even adopted orphaned or unwanted European children and raised them as their own.

A group of 19th-century Micmacs with their Roman Catholic priest. The people all wear clothing of wool and silk, decorated with ribbons and glass beads. The background design is a closeup of a box lid of quillwork on birchbark, of the kind the women made to sell.

During the 20th century, the health of the people has gradually improved and the population has been increasing. Although economic opportunities on reserves are few, the people are beginning to take control of their own lives and the affairs of their communities. **About 10,000 Micmac people live in the Maritime provinces today, in much the same region as did their ancestors.** Some have also settled in the United States or in other parts of Canada. Many of them still speak the Micmac language in their homes, but all now speak English or French as well. Their life is much like that of other Canadians. There are important differences, however. One is that of all the people who now call the Maritimes home, it is the Micmac whose ancestors have been here the longest – more than a thousand years before Cabot or Cartier. They remember this long heritage, and are proud.

Dr. Harold Franklin McGee, Jr. is an anthropologist at Saint Mary's University, Halifax, Nova Scotia; and editor of *The Native Peoples of Atlantic Canada*. (McClelland and Stewart 1974). He has published a number of articles in scientific journals on Micmac society and culture.

Ruth Holmes Whitehead is Curatorial Assistant in History at the Nova Scotia Museum, Halifax; and the author of *Micmac Quillwork* and *Elitekey: Micmac Material Culture From 1600 A.D. to the Present*. (N.S. Museum 1982, 1980)

Kathy R. Kaulbach is a graphic designer at the Nova Scotia Museum, responsible for print and publication design for the education section; she also does freelance work in publication design. This is her first work as an illustrator.

The illustrations for this book were taken from items in the Nova Scotia Museum collections; and from photographs by Ronald E. Merrick and Linda Wood made during the taping of *Mi'kmaq*. The authors were researchers and special consultants for this television series on 15th-century Micmac life, a 1981 co-production of the Nova Scotia Department of Education, CBC Halifax and the Micmac Association for Cultural Studies.